MUNCHEE'S FIRST CHRISTMAS IN HIS NEW HOUSE

Glynna Alderman Hood

Illustrated by Jesús Román

ISBN 979-8-88644-438-4 (Paperback)
ISBN 979-8-88644-440-7 (Hardcover)
ISBN 979-8-88644-439-1 (Digital)

Covenant Books
11661 Hwy 707
Murrells Inlet, SC 29576
www.covenantbooks.com

Thank you to my family and friends for your love and support and for
encouraging me to continue to write.

Thank you Jesús for the beautiful pictures. You
continue to amaze me with your talent.

Thank you to my cousin Bonnie Balliet Wilson for your words
of encouragement and for being my number one fan.

It's Munchee's first Christmas in his new house,
Sharing it with family and friends;
He's one happy mouse.

He decides to throw
a big celebration
And use his barn because
it's the biggest location.

"Where do I start!" Munchee said to himself.
"I need to enlist my family and friends and ask for some help!"

Munchee asked everyone to meet him at his barn
So he could tell them about his party plans down on the farm.

"I want to have a Christmas party, and I don't know where to start."
"I know Texas. Can we use your cart?"

"Count on me, Munchee," said Texas the Horse.
"I will pull my cart around and give free rides, of course!"

"Put me down," said Maple the Mouse.
"I make the best cheese pies, the best in the South!"

"I'll decorate the tables," said Shirley the Sheep.
"With red ribbons and red bows.
It will surely be chic!"

"I can provide all the milk," said Buttercup the Cow.
"I'll start making fresh cream for the pies right now!"

Oscar the Owl said,
"I can string the lights!"
"I'll fly tree to tree, it will be quite the sight!"

"I'll provide all the honey," said Beatrice the Bee.
"The best part of it all,
I get it for free!"

"I'll string acorns for the tree," said Sheala the Squirrel.
"And try making acorn soup,
I'll give it a whirl!"

Grampa B (Beaver) said, "I'll chop down the tree!"
"It will be the fluffiest and biggest one, you just wait and see!"

"I'll bring corn on the cob," said Hugo the Pig.
"And make a special desert using the best figs!"

"I make the best carrot cake!" said Reba the Rabbit.
"I make a lot of them,
It's become quite the habit!"

Darcy the Duck said, "I can bake cookies, that's what I can do."
"And get the little ones involved and decorate them
And do some crafting too!"

"Thank you all so much!"
Said Munchee to everyone.
"This will be the best party ever."
"Each one of you are unique and so clever!"

The day finally came, and there's much to be done.
Everyone was busy, but they were having lots of fun.

The barn was decorated with Christmas décor,
And beautiful wreaths were hung on the doors.

The tree was decorated
from head to toe
With strings of acorns and
red ribbons and bows.

The table was set with quite the spread,
Soups, veggies, cakes and pies,
And a big assortment of fresh baked breads.

The time came for the party to start.
Munchee knew all the hard work
came straight from the heart.

The little ones were busy decorating cookies with Darcy the Duck,
And they made wood ornaments and painted tiny toy trucks.

There were lots of dancing
out on the floor.
Munchee showed off his
dance moves, and everyone
applauded for more.

Texas was busy pulling his cart around town
While Shirley and Sheala sang carols. It was a lovely sound.

23

Beatrice handed
out honey jars for
party favors,

And Buttercup was giving out her cream
recipe with all the different flavors.

25

Maple served her cheese pie while Reba served her carrot cake.
Both very proud of what they had baked.

Hugo chowed down on his corn on the cob.
He ate so much, he decided to go for a short jog.

Oscar kept a close eye on all the lights
To make sure they would keep shining bright.

28

Munchee asked
everyone to gather
around the tree
To listen to a story
from Grandpa B.

Grandpa B said, "This is a special time of year.
But the true meaning of Christmas is a message so clear."
"It's about a little baby who was born on Christmas Day,
And his mother, Mary, laid him in a manger full of hay."

Everyone listened to the Christmas story,
And they sang songs of praises and glory.

Munchee was so happy with
how everything turned out
And wanted to share what
Christmas was all about.

Munchee thanked everyone for coming to his house
To share love and joy with one happy mouse.

About the Author

Glynna Alderman Hood is a retired preschool teacher assistant and has always loved reading to children. She loves to journal, write poems, and she loves writing in general. She loves spending time with her family and friends, going on trips, crafting, cake decorating, and other hobbies. She was born and raised, and still lives, in Sanford, Florida. This is her second published book.